Investigate

World Cultures

Louise Spilsbury

Heinemann Library
Chicago, Illinois

www.heinemannraintree.com
Visit our website to find out
more information about
Heinemann-Raintree books.

To order:

☎ Phone 888-454-2279

🖥 Visit www.heinemannraintree.com
to browse our catalog and order online.

Edited by Siân Smith, Rebecca Rissman, and Charlotte Guillain
Designed by Joanna Hinton-Malivoire
Original illustrations © Capstone Global Library
Picture research by Elizabeth Alexander and Sally Cole
Originated by Modern Age Repro House Ltd
Printed and bound in China by Leo Paper Group

14 13 12 11 10
10 9 8 7 6 5 4 3 2 1

Library of Congress Cataloging-in-Publication Data
Spilsbury, Louise.
  World cultures / Louise Spilsbury.
    p. cm. – (Investigate geography)
  Includes bibliographical references and index.
  ISBN 978-1-4329-3471-2 (hc) – ISBN 978-1-4329-3479-8 (pb) 1.
Ethnology–Juvenile literature. I. Title.
  GN333.S65 2009
  306–dc22
                                2009011045

Acknowledgments
The author and publishers are grateful to the following for
permission to reproduce copyright material: Alamy pp. **17** (©
Chris McLennan), **23**, **24** & **30** (© Greenshoots Communications),
27 (© John Bentley); Corbis pp. **5** (© Michele Westmorland), **6** (©
Arvind Garg), **7** (© James Marshall), **8** (© Bob Krist), **10** (© Earl
& Nazima Kowall), **11** (© Neil Emmerson/Robert Harding World
Imagery), **14** (© Martin Harvey), **15** (© Wendy Stone), **18** (© China
Newsphoto/Reuters), **19** (© Brijesh Singh/Reuters), **28** (© Pascal
Manoukian/Sygma), **30** (© Arvind Garg); Getty Images pp. **4**
(Adam Crowley/The Image Bank), **20** (Arif Ali/AFP); iStockphoto
pp. **29** & **30** (© Jani Bryson); Photolibrary pp. **12** (Klaus-Peter Wolf/
F1 Online), **13** (Atlantide SN.C/Age Fotostock), **16** (Ken Gillham/
Robert Harding Travel), **21** (Angelo Cavalli/Age Fotostock), **22**
(David Lomax/Robert Harding Travel), **25** (Marco Simoni/ Robert
Harding Travel).

Cover photograph of Lakhon and Khon dancers in traditional
clothing reproduced with permission of © Steven Vidler/
Eurasia Press.

Every effort has been made to contact copyright holders of
material reproduced in this book. Any omissions will be rectified in
subsequent printings if notice is given to the publishers.

Contents

People and Places. 4

Foods of the World. 6

Games and Leisure 10

Dressing Up 14

Celebrations and Religious Festivals 18

Houses and Homes 22

A Global Community. 26

Checklist 30

Glossary. 31

Index 32

Some words are shown in bold, **like this**. You can find out what they mean by looking in the glossary.

People and Places

All people in the world have the same basic needs. We all need food and water to live. We all need a home. We share these things with family and friends, and with other people who care about us.

There are also some differences between us. People from different **cultures** may wear different clothes. They may eat different foods and celebrate different festivals. People in different cultures can have different **religions** and **traditions**.

Foods of the World

Sharing meals is an important part of life for almost every **culture**. People eat different kinds of food because of what grows well in their **climate**. Some cultures eat particular foods because of their **traditions**.

 Corn is the **staple** food of most Mexicans. They use it to make thin, flat breads called tortillas.

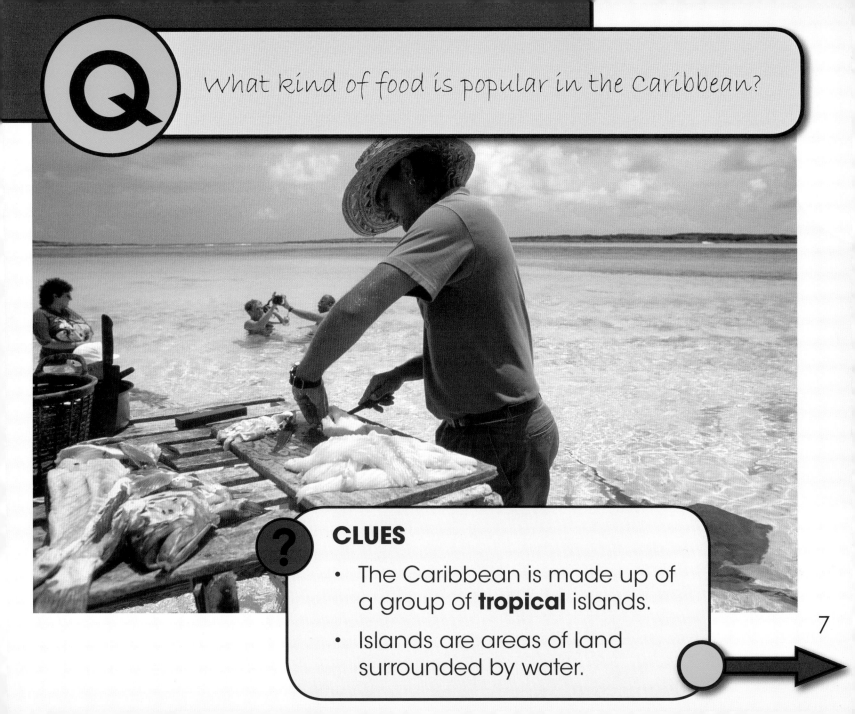

CLUES

- The Caribbean is made up of a group of **tropical** islands.

- Islands are areas of land surrounded by water.

7

A Fish and other kinds of seafood are popular in the Caribbean. People catch them from the sea around the islands.

People in the Caribbean eat **tropical** fruits and spices, too. Tropical areas are hot and damp all year. These are perfect conditions for growing spices and tropical fruits.

People may eat different foods because of their **religion**. For example, most **Buddhists** do not eat any meat. **Hindus** do not eat any beef.

Religious group	Pork	Beef	Lamb	Chicken	Fish
Hindu	✓	X	✓	✓	✓
Muslim	X	halal	halal	halal	✓
Sikh	X	X	✓	✓	✓
Jewish	X	kosher	kosher	kosher	no shellfish
Buddhist	X	X	X	X	X

 "Halal" and "kosher" mean meat from animals that has been prepared following **Muslim** and **Jewish** laws.

Games and Leisure

People play different sports in different places. For example, people play football mainly in the United States. Some games are played all over the world. Many people play simple games using stones, string, or sticks.

⬆ These children in Nepal are enjoying a game that involves tossing and catching small stones.

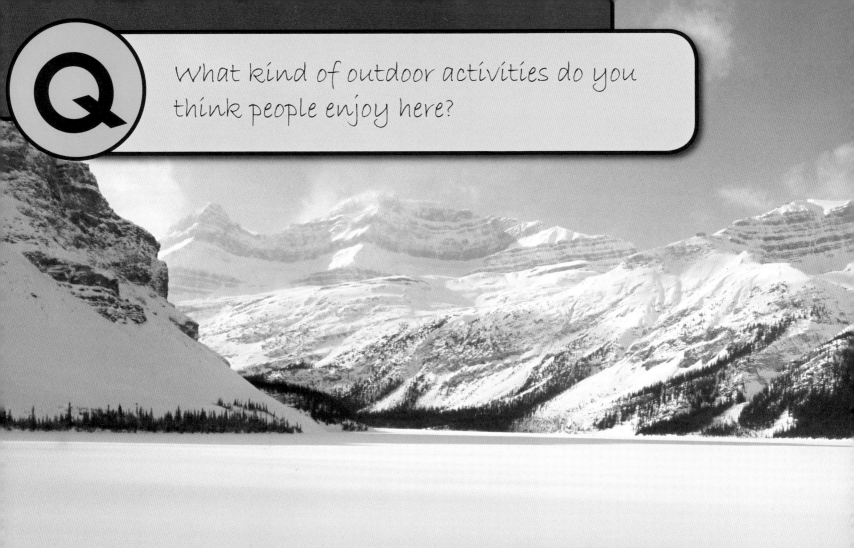

Q What kind of outdoor activities do you think people enjoy here?

 CLUE

• The outdoor activities people enjoy depend on their local **climate**.

11

A In cold, snowy places like Switzerland and Canada, people ski or sled on snow. They also ice-skate on frozen lakes.

Some families do not have money to buy toys. Many children around the world make toys out of whatever they can find. They may turn a scrap of plastic and some string into a kite.

→ These boys from Mozambique have made racing cars from old cardboard boxes and tin cans.

Dressing Up

Many people across the world wear similar clothes, such as jeans and T-shirts. Some **cultures** wear different kinds of clothing. These may be suited to their country's **climate** or their **religion**. Some people only wear **traditional** clothes on special occasions.

? CLUE

- The girls only wear this outfit on weekdays.

15

A The **Muslim** girls on page 15 wear this uniform when they go to school. Many children across the world wear school uniforms. Uniforms can make people feel part of the school **community**.

During the evening and on weekends, the girls wear their own clothes.

16

In Egypt the summer is very hot, and the Sun can burn people's skin quickly. Many people there wear long, flowing robes and scarves around their heads. The robes protect their bodies from the Sun. Also, most Egyptians are Muslims who believe in keeping their bodies covered in public.

17

Celebrations and Religious Festivals

Communities join together for celebrations all around the world. People sing special songs, eat special foods, and make decorations or give gifts. Some **cultures** celebrate changing seasons or special **religious** festivals.

Many people in the Chinese culture celebrate Chinese New Year with colorful, noisy fireworks.

Can you guess which **Hindu** festival these girls are celebrating?

CLUE
- What are they floating on the river?

They are celebrating the festival of lights. It is called Diwali. Small lamps called **diwas** are placed in rivers, doorways, windows, stores, and streets.

Hindu tradition says that diwa lamps help the goddess Lakshmi find people's homes. Some people believe that Lakshmi brings good luck. At Diwali people give gifts, eat special meals, and set off fireworks.

Lent is a time in spring when some **Christians** give up certain foods and spend time praying. A carnival is a last party before Lent begins. In carnivals people dress up in colorful costumes and masks. They play music and parade down the streets dancing.

These people are at a carnival in Rio de Janeiro, Brazil.

Houses and Homes

Homes are where people and families eat, sleep, and share time together. Today, many people live in similar types of homes. But some **cultures** have different kinds of homes.

Bedouin people often live in towns during winter. In summer many return to a **traditional** way of life and live in tents.

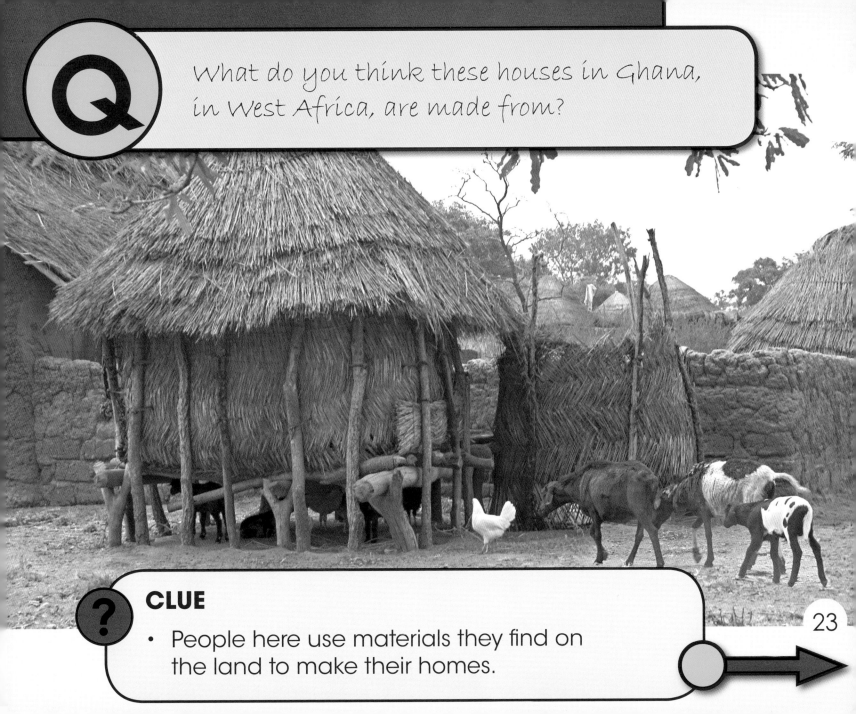

Q What do you think these houses in Ghana, in West Africa, are made from?

CLUE

- People here use materials they find on the land to make their homes.

23

A The walls of the houses are made from mud and the roofs are made from grass.

→ The homes are built in a circle so the **community** can live and work together.

In some places, people build houses to keep them warm or cool. In Finland, where it can be very cold, most homes have saunas. People warm up in these special heated rooms. On Greek islands, summers can be very hot. Many houses are white because this color keeps heat away.

↑ These houses are in the village of Oia, in Greece.

A Global Community

We are all part of the global **community**. We have connections with different countries of the world in many ways. For example, we rely on **tropical** countries for fruit like bananas. The farmers who grow the fruit need the money they earn by selling them to us.

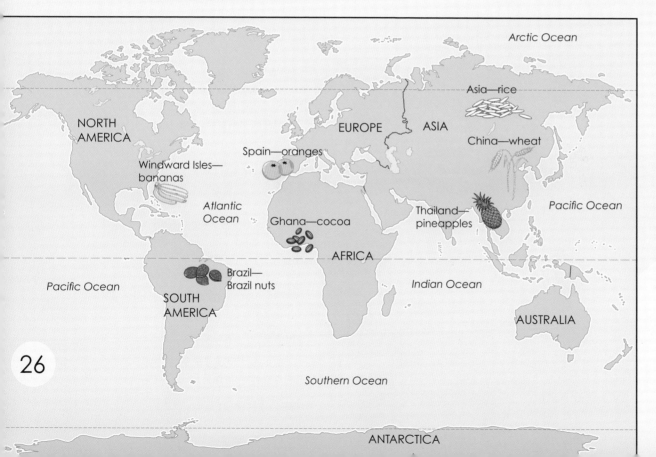

The banana is just one food we eat that comes from around the world. This map shows some of the food provided by different countries.

Reggae music originally came from Jamaica.

We do not just share or exchange food and other products with other places. Much of the music we listen to first began in other places, too. What else can you think of that has come from other countries?

People in all **cultures** are equal. We all have the same basic **rights**. All children have the right:

⇒ to be free and safe

⇒ to go to school and learn

⇒ to have time and space to play

⇒ to have love and understanding.

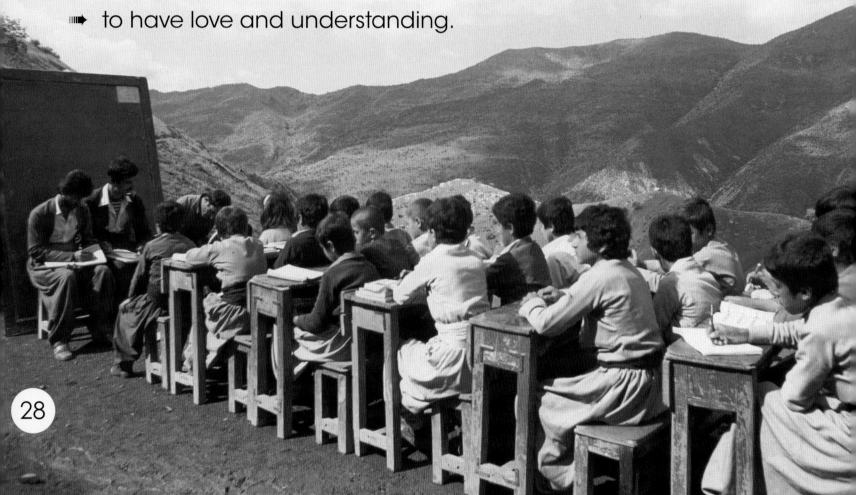

It is important to learn about different cultures. It shows us that our lives are different in some ways, but that we have much in common. When we understand how we are similar and why we are different, people can live together and show each other **respect**.

Checklist

People around the world are different in some ways. This is often because of the **religion**, **traditions**, and **climate** in the places they live.

⟫ People wear different clothes.

⟫ People eat different foods.

⟫ People follow different religions.

⟫ People celebrate different festivals.

But we are all the same in many important ways. We share the same basic needs. We all need:

food and water
to survive

somewhere
to live

family and
friends

Glossary

Buddhist person who follows the teachings of Buddha

Christian person who follows the teachings of Christ

climate usual pattern of weather in a country over a year

community group of people who live in the same place or have something in common

culture arts, customs, beliefs, and values that make a community special

diwa small candle or lamp Hindus light for Diwali, the festival of light

Hindu person who follows Hinduism

Jewish person who follows the Jewish religion

Muslim person who follows the religion of Islam

religion People following a religion usually believe in a god or gods. Different religious groups believe different things and worship in different ways.

respect consider and value a person's feelings and opinions

right something people are entitled to. We all have a right to be safe and to be treated with respect, for example.

staple basic or essential food

tradition way of behaving that has been part of a culture or community for many years

tropical region of the world that has a hot, rainy climate

Index

Buddhists 9

carnivals 21
celebrations 18–21, 30
Christians 21
climates 6, 11, 14, 30
clothes 5, 14–17, 30
communities 16, 18, 24,
  26–27

foods 5, 6–9, 26, 30

games and leisure 10–13
global community 26–27

Hindus 9, 19–20
houses and homes 22–25

Jews 9

music 27
Muslims 9, 16, 17

religions 5, 9, 14, 18–21, 30
respect 29
rights 28

Sikhs 9

toys 13
traditions 5, 6, 14, 20,
  22, 30
tropical areas 7–8, 26